The Chief Data Officer Handbook
for Data Governance

Sunil Soares

MC Press Online, LLC

Boise, ID 83703 USA

The Chief Data Officer Handbook for Data Governance
Sunil Soares

First Edition

© Copyright 2014 Sunil Soares. All rights reserved.

MC Press Online, LLC

Corporate Offices:
3695 W. Quail Heights Court, Boise, ID 83703-3861 USA

Sales and Customer Service:
(208) 629-7275 ext. 500; service@mcpressonline.com

Permissions and Bulk/Special Orders:
mcbooks@mcpressonline.com

www.mcpressonline.com • www.mc-store.com

ISBN: 978-1-58347-417-4   WB201412

About the Author

Sunil Soares is the founder and managing partner of Information Asset, a consulting firm that specializes in data governance. Prior to this role, Sunil was director of information governance at IBM, where he worked with clients across six continents and multiple industries.

This is Sunil's sixth book about data governance. His first book, *The IBM Data Governance Unified Process* (MC Press, 2010), details the almost 100 steps to implement a data governance program. This book has been used by several organizations as the blueprint for their data governance programs and has been translated into Chinese. Sunil's second book, *Selling Information Governance to the Business: Best Practices by Industry and Job Function* (MC Press, 2011), reviews the best practices to approach information governance by industry and function. His third book, *Big Data Governance* (MC Press, 2012), addresses the specific issues associated with the governance of big data; it, too, has been translated into Chinese. His fourth book, *IBM InfoSphere: A Platform for Big Data Governance and Process Data Governance* (MC Press, 2013), also deals with the governance of big data. His fifth book, *Data Governance Tools* (MC Press, 2014), addresses how critical data governance tasks can be automated using tools.

Prior to joining IBM, Sunil consulted with major financial institutions at the Financial Services Strategy Consulting Practice of Booz Allen & Hamilton in New York. Sunil lives in New Jersey and holds an MBA in Finance and Marketing from the University of Chicago Booth School of Business.

Contents

Foreword.. ix

Preface... xi

Chapter 1: Ingredients for Data Governance Success....................1

Summary...3

Chapter 2: The CDO Agenda 5

Summary...9

Chapter 3: Organizing for Data Governance...........................11

Agree on the Reporting Relationship for the Chief Data Officer 11

Determine the Level of Centralization of the Chief Data Office 13

Define the Overall Scope of the Chief Data Office 16

Establish Overall Funding and Decision-Making Authority 19

Enlist the Chief Information Officer as a Strong Partner..................20

Appoint a Data Governance Lead...21

Establish a Data Governance Program Office 21

Summary..22

Chapter 4: Driving Business Ownership of Data........................23

Build a Stakeholder Map 24

Agree on the Responsibilities of the Data Owner............................25

Compile a List of Applications, Data Repositories, and Datasets
Across the Enterprise 26

Identify Data Owners Who Are Willing and Able
to Be Accountable for Data Within Their Purview............................26

Obtain Buy-In from Data Owners That They Are Accountable
for the Trustworthiness of Data Under Their Ownership 28

Agree with Data Owners That They Are Accountable
for Supporting Security and Privacy Relative to Data Under
Their Ownership 28

Ensure That Data Owners Appoint Business Data Stewards to
Manage Data on a Day-to-Day Basis..29

Work with the CIO So That Technical Data Stewards Are
Accountable for the Data Infrastructure 31

Identify Operational Data Stewards..33

Summary..33

Chapter 5: Setting Data Policies, Standards, and Processes.......35

Prescribe Terminology for Data Policies...35

Establish a Framework for Data Policies...36

Data Quality Management Policy..37

Metadata Management Policy..39

Reference Data Management Policy...40

Email Address Policy..42

Facebook Data Policy 42

Establish Process for Data Policy Changes 42

Summary..44

Chapter 6: Monitoring Data Governance....................................45

Select Data Policies, Standards, and Processes to Be Included
Within the Dashboard 45

Pick the Data Repositories to Be Included Within the Dashboard ...46

Identify Data Owners for Each Policy, Standard, Repository,
and Overall..47

Score Each Data Repository by Data Standard................................48

Circulate the Data Governance Dashboard on a Periodic Basis 48

Summary...48

Chapter 7: Enforcing Data Governance 51

Determine the Overall Approach to Enforce Data Policies,
Standards, and Processes 51

Validate Auditability of Data Policies, Standards, and Processes 52

Support Efforts to Audit the Compliance with Data Policies,
Standards, and Processes 52

Review Deviations from Data Policies, Standards, and Processes ...54

Summary...54

**Chapter 8: Building a Successful Technology Foundation
for Data Governance 55**

Summary...57

Appendix A: Acronyms...59

Appendix B: Glossary..61

**Appendix C: Key Data Governance Activities on the Agenda
of the Chief Data Officer 67**

Foreword

Since 2006, I have created the role of Chief Data Officer thrice in different healthcare organizations. My role expanded in scope over time, in keeping with the trend of increasing importance of data to a business. I went from the leader of a functional unit to the general manager of a business unit and then to a member of the CEO's senior leadership team. I had to reinvent the CDO role at each transition to reflect the expanded scope. But one aspect remained constant: Every time, I had to implement a data governance program.

Why was that the case? The CDO has to change the culture of the organization. While once data was viewed as a byproduct of the business, it now has to be treated as an important corporate asset. What does that entail, and how should it be done?

Changing the culture of a large organization is about the most challenging of corporate assignments one can undertake. You have to win the hearts and minds of your fellow workers at all levels—no easy task. The key to simplifying that task and to effecting change is a formal data governance program. Let me explain why.

To be lasting, a culture change must be worked in every possible way. Otherwise, a large organization will not let it take hold. The implementation of a data governance program enables such a multipronged approach. For example, we must establish a structure for data stewardship as part of data governance, so that those who are working with data understand the importance of their role and ensure that data are accurate and reliable. Stewardship is a bottom-up approach to changing the culture of the organization.

We must also establish a governance council that meets regularly and is composed of representatives from business, legal, and information technology—all of whom are needed to set policy and enforce it on matters pertaining to data. This structure cuts across organizational boundaries. It is a lateral approach to changing the culture.

Most important, we must make sure the data governance program is adequately funded by securing the sponsorship of the senior leaders of the organization. Once they become sponsors of the data governance program, these leaders direct their departments to participate in the program. This is a top-down approach to changing the culture.

When implemented appropriately, data governance is a powerful framework. It enables the right messages around data to be carried throughout the organization simultaneously along all possible pathways of communication. It makes it simpler to change the culture of how data are managed.

So how does a CDO implement data governance appropriately? First, read this book. Sunil is a pioneer in the field. Through his clear and pithy writing, he has made the art form of data governance into a science. Second, educate your team by having *them* read this book. In this remarkably short guide, Sunil has gone a step further by reducing the science to a formula. It is a quick read and yet a comprehensive treatment of the subject. Third, implement data governance. Using a prescriptive, step-by-step approach, Sunil explains how to do so. I recommend you follow that prescription to success.

Inderpal Bhandari
Chief Data Officer
Cambia Health

Preface

The Chief Data Officer (CDO) is a C-level role with overall account-ability for data as an enterprise asset. Although the CDO role is still evolving, various aspects are becoming more settled. For example, the CDO increasingly reports into the business. In addition, data governance is perceived as a critical function as part of the chief data office. Finally, other executives increasingly view the CDO as the go-to person for data-related issues within the company.

Data governance is the formulation of policy to optimize, secure, and leverage information as an enterprise asset by aligning the objectives of multiple functions. This book explores the critical relationship between the CDO and the data governance team.

The book consists of the following chapters:

1. *Ingredients for Data Governance Success*

   A review of the five key ingredients of data governance success

2. *The CDO Agenda*

   A discussion about the key drivers of the CDO role, including the regulatory environment, data monetization, big data, and data politics

3. *Organizing for Data Governance*

   A review of industry patterns around the CDO reporting relationship, the level of centralization and scope of the chief data office, the level of authority, and alignment with the CIO

4. *Driving Business Ownership of Data*

   A review of the CDO stakeholder map, data owners, business data stewards, technical data stewards, and operational data stewards

5. *Setting Data Policies, Standards, and Processes*

   A tutorial on data policies, standards, and processes, including some examples for data quality, metadata, reference data, email address, and Facebook® data

6. *Monitoring Data Governance*

A primer on the use of data governance dashboards to monitor adherence to data policies, standards, and processes

7. *Enforcing Data Governance*

A review of the different approaches to enforcing compliance with data governance, including data audits and alignment with internal audit

8. *Building a Successful Technology Foundation for Data Governance*

A description of how Informatica's market-leading platform for enterprise data management provides a strong foundation for data governance

The book is geared toward business users and is non-technical in nature. Sample roles who might be interested in this book include the following:

- Chief Data Officer

- Senior Vice President of Enterprise Data Management

- Vice President of Enterprise Data Management

- Senior Vice President of Enterprise Information Management

- Vice President of Enterprise Information Management

- Chief Operating Officer

- Chief Risk Officer

- Chief Information Officer

- Chief Marketing Officer

- Chief Executive Officer

1

Ingredients for Data Governance Success

DATA GOVERNANCE IS THE FORMULATION OF POLICY TO optimize, secure, and leverage information as an enterprise asset by aligning the objectives of multiple functions. By its very nature, data governance requires cross-departmental cooperation to deliver timely, trustworthy data for better decisions.

Many organizations have tried and failed to implement successful data governance programs. Having reviewed the characteristics of hundreds of data governance programs, we have developed five ingredients of a successful data governance program:

1. *Strong business ownership with IT support*

   Successful data governance programs are owned by the business with strong IT support. Nascent data governance programs may start in IT, but they need to move into the business once they have achieved a level of maturity. Strong business ownership requires executive sponsorship around clearly defined business problems. For example, the chief risk officer in a bank may be the executive sponsor to improve the trustworthiness of data for Basel II compliance. The chief financial officer may also sponsor data governance to improve the quality of financial reporting. It goes without saying that strong executive sponsorship will ensure the appropriate level of funding and staffing for the data governance program. IT is also an important ingredient of data governance success. As we discuss in Chapter 8, technology plays a critical role in the successful implementation of a data governance program.

2. *Focus on critical data elements*

   Because it is impossible to successfully govern all the data across the enterprise, mature data governance programs must focus on critical data elements (CDEs). These are a handful of attributes that have a significant impact on regulatory reporting, operational performance, and business intelligence.

3. *Emphasis on data artifacts*

   Successful data governance programs generate a number of valuable data artifacts. These data artifacts include business terms, business rules, code tables, policies, standards, processes, data quality scorecards, and data issues. Over time, successful data governance programs generate a rhythm associated with the production and approval of these artifacts at meetings of the data stewards and the data governance council.

4. *Alignment around metrics and policy enforcement*

   As with any program, data governance must focus on metrics that are important to the business. These metrics may be "the number of critical data elements with end-to-end data lineage" or the data quality index. Successful data governance programs also introduce mechanisms to enforce data policies, standards, and processes. These mechanisms include data governance scorecards, escalations, and data audits.

5. *Celebration of quick wins with alignment around the long-term roadmap*

   Successful data governance programs are able to point to quick wins within weeks of inception. These quick wins may be creation of a glossary for key business terms or a data quality report. However, these programs are also tied into a long-term roadmap over 12 to 18 months.

As you can imagine, it is not easy to implement data governance successfully. Many organizations have tried, and many have failed. As we discuss in the next chapter, data governance councils often lack the clout to successfully align the different factions in an organization. The Chief Data Officer (CDO) is a recent innovation to create a strong executive focus on data governance.

Summary

In this chapter, we introduced the importance of the CDO to the successful implementation of a data governance program. The five ingredients of data governance success are strong business ownership with IT support, focus on critical data elements, emphasis on data artifacts, alignment around metrics and policy enforcement, and celebration of quick wins with alignment around the long-term roadmap.

2

The CDO Agenda

MANY COMPANIES HAVE ESTABLISHED CENTRALIZED DATA management departments. These departments are variously referred to as "enterprise data management," "enterprise information management," or the "chief data office." Whatever they are called, these departments share some common characteristics. They have accountability for data as an enterprise asset, and they increasingly report into the business. The leader of these departments often carries the title of vice president of enterprise data management, senior vice president of enterprise data management, vice president of enterprise information management, or senior vice president of enterprise information management. Increasingly, these leaders are being anointed as Chief Data Officers.

We will first define certain foundational terms for this book:

- *Enterprise Data Management (EDM)* refers to the ability of an organization to precisely define, easily integrate, and effectively retrieve data for both internal applications and external communication.[1] EDM includes a number of disciplines, such as data governance, data ownership, data architecture, data modeling, data integration, database management and operations, data security and privacy, master data management, reference data management, data warehousing, critical data elements, metadata management, data quality management, information lifecycle management, and content management.

- *Enterprise Information Management (EIM)* is synonymous with EDM.

---

[1] http://en.wikipedia.org/wiki/Enterprise_data_management

- The *Chief Data Officer* is a C-level executive with overall accountability for EDM.

- The *chief data office* refers to the EDM organization or department, which reports to the CDO.

- *Data governance* is the formulation of policy to optimize, secure, and leverage information as an enterprise asset by aligning the objectives of multiple functions. Data governance is a discipline under EDM.

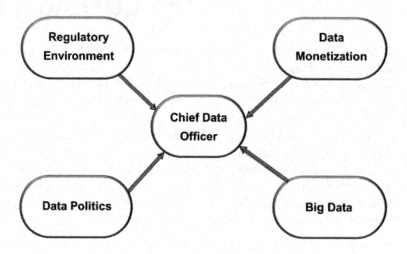

Figure 2.1: The emergence of the Chief Data Officer

The emergence of the CDO is driven by four macro-trends as shown in Figure 2.1:

1. *Regulatory environment*

    Many companies, especially those in the financial services industry, must comply with stringent regulations that are data-centric in nature. Banks must comply with regulations such as the Basel Committee on Banking Supervision (BCBS) 239 for risk data aggregation and the Dodd-Frank Wall Street Reform and Consumer Protection Act. Insurers need to comply with regulations that include Solvency II in Europe as well as directives from regulators in each state in the United States. Broker-dealers must comply with regulations from the Financial Industry Regulatory Authority (FINRA). Many federal, state, and local governments also have CDOs to lead their open data initiatives so that citizens can freely access data without any encumbrances. Because data is critical to regulatory compliance, these companies have identified their CDOs as the single focal point to handle data-related issues. In other words, the CDO is answerable to the regulators if the data is not trustworthy.

2. *Data monetization*

   Data monetization is the process of deriving quantifiable business value from information. The C-suites in large companies increasingly recognize the tremendous value of data. This has spawned an entire generation of analytics departments that are geared toward data monetization initiatives. However, these initiatives have to be tempered by the acceptable use of data in the light of regulatory compliance, privacy concerns, brand reputation, and contractual restrictions. The CDO often has overall responsibility for the tradeoffs between data monetization and acceptable use concerns.

3. *Big data*

   Big data has highlighted a number of new data sources, including sensors, social media, web cookies, and data brokers. It has also driven new technologies such as Hadoop® and NoSQL. The traditional IT departments may not be familiar with these technologies. In addition, the corporate security and privacy departments may be playing catch-up with the latest developments around big data. Once again, the CDO may be asked to lead the overall big data initiative.

4. *Data politics*

   Companies have always grappled with the differing business priorities of data producers and data consumers. We refer to this dynamic as "data politics." As discussed in Case Study 2.1 (on page 8), data governance councils have sought to align the competing business objectives of multiple business areas. However, these data governance councils have had mixed success due to their lack of political clout. The rise of the CDO is an effort to add some level of centralized control over data as an enterprise asset.

Case Study 2.1: Data politics around phone number at a retailer[2]

In some states in the United States, retailers incent store associates to capture phone numbers at the point of sale. Phone numbers create an interesting political dynamic between store operations and marketing. Marketing depends on high-quality phone numbers to improve customer insight. Even if the customer pays in cash, marketing can do a "reverse append" to obtain the customer ID based on the phone number. Marketing can then use the customer ID to add the customer's purchases to their overall transaction history in the data warehouse. Store operations needs to train and incent the store associates to capture accurate phone numbers at the point of sale. However, some customers will decline to provide a phone number. In addition, some store associates try to meet their targets by entering the phone number of the store or a local hotel. As part of the chief data office, the data governance team must work with marketing and store operations to establish real-time validation rules to ensure that store associates enter appropriate phone numbers at the point of sale. The CDO must have enough political clout to align the competing objectives of store operations and marketing.

Data governance is critical to the success of the CDO. The following data governance topics are key to the CDO agenda:

- How do we organize for data governance?

- How do we drive business ownership of data?

- How do we set data policies, standards, and processes?

- How do we monitor the adherence to these data policies, standards, and processes?

- How do we enforce the compliance with these data policies, standards, and processes?

- How do we leverage technology, especially in the context of big data?

The remainder of this book will review each of these topics in detail.

---

[2] Adapted from *Selling Information Governance to the Business* (Sunil Soares, MC Press, 2011).

Summary

In this chapter, we reviewed the key trends that are driving the emergence of the CDO. These trends include the regulatory environment, data monetization, big data, and data politics. Companies are awakening to the realization that data is the lifeblood of the organization and it needs to be dealt with appropriately. The chief data office is often tasked with establishing data as a key business differentiator by discovering valuable data, defining data policies, and managing the trustworthiness of the data as an asset.

3

Organizing
for Data Governance

ALTHOUGH THE CDO ROLE IS STILL EVOLVING, A NUMBER
of organizational patterns are already beginning to emerge. Companies
must recognize these organizational patterns to maximize the likelihood
of CDO success. These topics are discussed in this chapter.

Agree on the Reporting Relationship for the Chief Data Officer

There is no one single answer to where the CDO should report. This
section is based on the reporting patterns that exist today. However, we
anticipate that these reporting patterns will become standardized as more
companies appoint CDOs. Today's CDO may report to a number of
executives as discussed below.

- *Chief Information Officer*

  The CDO most commonly reports to the Chief Information
  Officer (CIO). Because there is no logical "Switzerland" or
  supposedly unbiased party that has a strong interest in data, the
  default reporting structure for the CDO is the CIO. This structure
  also eliminates any potential conflicts between the CDO and the
  rest of the IT department. However, this structure may reinforce
  the perception that data is owned by IT and is not a business
  problem.

- *Chief Operating Officer*

  An increasing number of companies have the CDO reporting to
  the Chief Operating Officer (COO). This reporting structure has
  a few key advantages. First, the COO may be perceived to be the

"Switzerland," or impartial arbiter, of data as an enterprise asset. As a result, marketing, sales, finance, and other functions will be more inclined to accept the role of the CDO. Second, the COO already has a key focus on operational efficiency. This reporting structure reinforces the COO's key mission by leveraging data to improve operating efficiency. In one instance, a large bank had both the CIO and the CDO as direct reports to the COO.

- *Chief Executive Officer or President*

  The CDO may also report to the Chief Executive Officer (CEO) or President of the company. This reporting structure works well in information services companies, which aggregate information for sale to customers. It may also work well in situations where there is a heightened level of focus on information as an enterprise asset. The downside is that the CEO or President may not always have the time to devote to the CDO.

- *Chief Risk Officer*

  The CDO may also report to the Chief Risk Officer (CRO). This reporting structure works very well in industries such as banking and insurance that have a strong risk management focus. However, other functions, such as marketing, sales, product management, and finance, may feel shortchanged.

- *Chief Financial Officer*

  The CDO may also report to the Chief Financial Officer (CFO). This reporting structure works very well in industries such as manufacturing or in companies that are finance-driven. Other functions, however, such as marketing, sales, product management, and risk management, may feel less connected to the EDM program.

- *Chief Marketing Officer*

  The CDO may also report to the Chief Marketing Officer (CMO). This reporting structure works very well in in companies with a strong focus on customer-oriented marketing and analytics. However, the non-marketing functions may feel less aligned with the CDO in this reporting structure.

Although there is no right or wrong answer, companies must adopt the following criteria when determining the appropriate reporting structure for the CDO:

- *Size of company*—The CDO may report to a more senior executive in smaller companies. However, the CDO may report a few levels down from the CEO in very large companies.

- *Executive champion*—The CDO should report to the senior executive who champions the use of data as an enterprise asset. This executive may be the CRO, CFO, CMO, or somebody else.

- *Level of business sponsorship*—If a company has limited business sponsorship for EDM, it will likely struggle with the CDO role. In this case, it is advisable to have the CDO report to the CIO on an interim basis. Once the business starts to see value from EDM, the CDO can move into the business.

Determine the Level of Centralization of the Chief Data Office

The organization must also determine the level of centralization of the chief data office. We discuss a number of patterns for the chief data office below:

- *Single, Centralized Chief Data Office*

  The first pattern is a single, centralized chief data office. This model works well for smaller companies that operate in a single geography and a single product line.

- *Federated Chief Data Office by Geography*

  Larger organizations may adopt a federated approach by geography. As shown in Figure 3.1, a multinational corporation may adopt a federated model with a global CDO as well as regional CDOs for the Americas, Europe, and Asia Pacific. The regional CDOs report into their respective regions but are dotted line to the global CDO. This approach addresses some of the political realities inherent in the fact that most organizations are not ready to completely centralize their data-related decision-making. The geographically federated model also allows data decisions to be made closer to the revenue-generating regions.

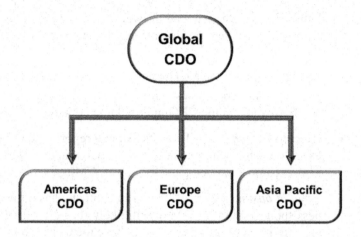

Figure 3.1: Federated chief data office by geography

- *Federated Chief Data Office by Business Unit*

  Some organizations may also adopt a federated approach by business unit, as shown in Figure 3.2. The business unit CDOs report into their individual business units but are dotted line to the global CDO. This approach allows organizations to have some level of enterprise coordination but also permits data decisions to be close to the revenue-generating business units.

- *Federated Chief Data Office by Geography and Business Unit*

  Some companies may also adopt a hybrid approach, with a federated model by geography and business unit. As shown in Figure 3.3, a large multinational bank established a global CDO role. The Americas CDO had a dual role as the corporate banking CDO, while the Asia Pacific CDO was also the retail banking CDO. The geography CDOs reported into the regional organizations but were dotted line to the global CDO.

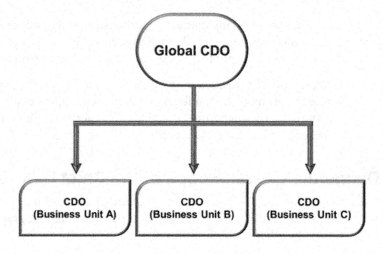

Figure 3.2: Federated chief data office by business unit

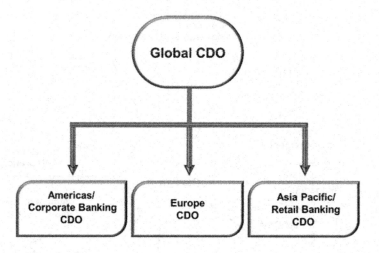

Figure 3.3: Federated chief data office by geography and business unit

Other approaches to the chief data office will likely emerge as the CDO role becomes more mainstream. Although there is no right or wrong answer, companies must adopt the following criteria when establishing the level of centralization of the chief data office:

- *Size of company*—Smaller companies may adopt a more centralized model.

- *Geographic dispersion*—Companies that operate across multiple geographies may adopt a federated model.

- *Product lines*—Companies with multiple product lines or business units may adopt a federated model, while those with single or homogeneous product lines may adopt a centralized model.

- *Organizational dynamics*—Companies with very strong department heads may adopt a federated approach. Others that have a culture of cross-department collaboration are more likely to succeed with a centralized approach.

Define the Overall Scope of the Chief Data Office

The organization must define the overall scope of the chief data office. As shown in Figure 3.4, data governance is a foundational program that ties together the other EDM disciplines.

Figure 3.4: Scope of the chief data office in terms of EDM disciplines

We discuss each EDM discipline below:

- *Data governance*—The formulation of policy to optimize, secure, and leverage information as an enterprise asset by aligning the objectives of multiple functions

- *Data ownership*—The process of identifying individuals who will be accountable for the trustworthiness and supporting security and privacy of data within their purview

- *Data architecture*—A discipline that sets data standards for data systems as a vision or a model of the eventual interactions between those data systems[1]

- *Data modeling*—The process of establishing data models, which use a set of symbols and text to precisely explain a subset of real information to improve communication within the organization and thereby lead to a more flexible and stable application environment[2]

- *Data integration*—A process that involves combining data from multiple sources to provide new insights to business users

- *Database management and operations*—The process of managing data repositories

- *Data security and privacy*—The process of avoiding unauthorized access to data

- *Master data management*—The process of establishing a single version of the truth for an organization's critical data entities, such as customers, products, materials, vendors, and chart of accounts

- *Reference data management*—The process of managing static data such as country codes, state or province codes, and industry classification codes, which may be placed in lookup tables for reference by other applications across the enterprise

- *Data warehousing*—The process of creating a centralized repository of data for reporting and analysis

---

[1] http://en.wikipedia.org/wiki/Data_architecture

[2] *Data Modeling Made Simple, 2nd Edition* (Steve Hoberman, Technics Publications, LLC, 2009).

- *Critical data elements*—Attributes that have a significant impact on regulatory reporting, operational performance, and business intelligence

- *Metadata management*—The management of information that describes the characteristics of any data artifact, such as its name, location, criticality, quality, business rules, and relationships to other data artifacts

- *Data quality management*—A discipline that includes methods to measure and improve the quality and integrity of an organization's data

- *Information lifecycle management*—The process and methodology of managing information through its lifecycle, from creation through disposal, including compliance with legal, regulatory, and privacy requirements

- *Content management*—The process of digitizing, collecting, and classifying paper and electronic documents

Companies must engage key stakeholders to scope out the CDO role. Based on current trends in the industry, there are a number of patterns for the scope of the chief data office:

- *Data governance focus*

  In this pattern, the CDO owns data governance as well as a limited set of functions, such as data quality and metadata. Other functions, such as data warehousing, master data management, reference data management, content management, data architecture, and data modeling, report to the CIO. In essence, the CDO establishes data policies and standards around EDM but outsources the technology aspects to the CIO.

- *Data governance plus some operational and analytical systems*

  In this pattern, the CDO owns data governance, data quality, and metadata as well as other functions such as master data management, reference data management, and data warehousing. However, the CIO still retains control over the other functions.

- *Broad EDM scope*

  In this pattern, the CDO owns most EDM functions, with the exception of some departments such as database management, which may continue to report to the CIO. The reporting structure for data architecture and data modeling is typically highly sensitive because it may involve breaking apart the enterprise architecture department.

As with any organization, discussions about reporting structures are fraught with political debate. The CDO must tread lightly because some or all of these functions would originally have resided within IT for decades before moving into the chief data office. There is no right or wrong answer. However, companies need to adopt the following criteria when defining the scope of the chief data office:

- How much autonomy do we want to afford the CDO?

- What role do we want the CIO to play with respect to EDM?

- How will the CIO feel if the scope of IT is significantly reduced?

- How important is it to have certain functions reporting to the CDO?

- Can certain functions remain in IT with a dotted line to the CDO?

- Can we attract the right CDO candidate with a reduced scope?

Establish Overall Funding and Decision-Making Authority

In the words of one CDO, "A CDO without the appropriate funding and decision-making authority risks becoming the officer of data pontification." This comment is somewhat flippant, but it underscores the fact that the CDO role is evolving. The following is a list of questions that every CDO must ask as he or she goes about the business:

- Will I have a team with the appropriate size and funding to drive the overall EDM initiative?

- What is the engagement model with IT and enterprise architecture in acquiring software tools?

  o Who defines the required functionality for software tools?

  o Who interfaces with software vendors?

  o Who gets to make the final decision?

o Can my team select and purchase software tools on their own? Will IT select and purchase software tools based on input from the chief data office?

o Will I have the budget to acquire software tools?

- Can I introduce data-related tollgates within the systems development lifecycle (SDLC)? Can I delay a project because data quality and metadata issues have not been appropriately addressed?

- Can I establish data policies, standards, and processes? Will these have any "teeth"?

- How can I work with internal audit to enforce compliance with data policies, standards, and processes?

- What is my role with regard to regulators? For example, several financial institutions leverage the chief data office to demonstrate compliance with data-related regulatory requirements or to close out audit findings relating to data.

Because the CDO role is still evolving, the CDO must clarify and define his or her responsibilities and organizational boundaries when first appointed.

Enlist the Chief Information Officer as a Strong Partner

CIO-level support is critical whether the CDO reports into IT or the business. Some organizations have an EDM department that reports two or more levels down from the CIO. In these situations, the CIO may not have the appropriate visibility into this department. As a result, the effectiveness of the department may suffer due to lack of funding and sponsorship.

CIO support is even more important if the chief data office reports into the business. In this case, functions such as data architecture and data modeling may have moved from IT into the CDO. If not handled properly, this transition has the potential to create friction between the CIO and the CDO. It is imperative that the CDO engage the CIO as a key partner and stakeholder in the success of the EDM initiative.

Appoint a Data Governance Lead

The CDO must appoint a data governance lead who will have day-to-day responsibility for the program. The responsibilities of the data governance lead include the following:

- Lead the data governance program office with broad oversight over the data governance program.

- Drive the documentation, approval, and operationalization of data policies, standards, and processes.

- Facilitate ongoing communication to executive stakeholders across the company.

- Manage alignment with data owners across the company.

- Oversee the activities of the business data stewards.

- Support data quality efforts, including the definition of business rules.

- Drive the metadata initiative, including the establishment of a business glossary.

- Facilitate the implementation of a master data program.

- Drive the reference data program.

- Work with the technology team to select and implement data governance tools.

- Develop a data governance dashboard to monitor adherence to data policies, standards, and processes.

- Work with internal audit to enforce compliance with data policies, standards, and processes.

Establish a Data Governance Program Office

The CDO must also fund a data governance program office that will drive the program on a daily basis. The program office may consist of a small team of business analysts who implement the data governance program. In some instances, the data governance program office may also consist of a dedicated team that conducts data audits to enforce compliance with data policies, standards, and processes. We discuss this topic in detail in Chapter 6 on enforcing data governance.

Summary

In this chapter, we reviewed the key organizational prerequisites of CDO success. Decisions must be made regarding the reporting relationship of the CDO, the level of centralization, and the scope of the chief data office. The CDO must have the right level of funding and decision-making authority. The CDO must enlist the CIO as a key partner. Finally, the CDO must identify the right data governance lead and establish a data governance program office.

4

Driving Business Ownership of Data

IN MANY ORGANIZATIONS, THE PRODUCERS AND CONSUMERS of the data reside in different departments. These departments have different requirements in terms of the data. The CDO must facilitate business ownership of data. Case Study 4.1 reviews the ownership of job classification codes at a life sciences company by data producers (human resources) and data consumers (manufacturing).

Case Study 4.1: Job classifications and product quality[1]

A life sciences company had a number of challenges around using correct job classification codes for new hires. For a variety of reasons, several new hires were improperly classified in the human resources application. As a result, these employees received incorrect training. The business outcome was an adverse impact on product quality and the potential risk of regulatory sanctions and fines. The data governance team, sponsored by the vice presidents of manufacturing and human resources, implemented a tight focus on improving the accuracy of employee job codes, which resulted in improvements in product quality.

In this chapter, we will discuss a list of steps that will facilitate the business ownership of data.

---

[1] Adapted from *Selling Information Governance to the Business* (Sunil Soares, MC Press, 2011).

Build a Stakeholder Map

The CDO must establish a map of key stakeholders who will have an impact on the overall success of the EDM initiative. The CDO must always ask the question, "How can my department help these executives achieve success?" The answer to this question will drive key initiatives.

As shown in Figure 4.1, these stakeholders may include the following roles:

- The *Chief Executive Officer* needs to understand and embrace the CDO's role in monetizing data and preserving the company's brand.

- *Business Unit Presidents* must view the CDO as a crucial partner to improve operating efficiencies and increase revenues based on EDM best practices.

- The *Chief Operating Officer* may well be the direct reporting manager of the CDO. In any event, the COO must view the CDO as a critical partner in using data to improve operating efficiencies.

- The *Chief Information Officer* may be the direct reporting manger of the CDO and needs to be a strong partner around EDM.

- The *Chief Financial Officer* must collaborate with the CDO on critical projects such as a business glossary to support financial reporting.

- The *Chief Human Resources Officer* is a critical ally as the CDO looks to create career paths for emerging roles such as the data steward.

- The *Chief Information Security Officer* and the CDO may co-sponsor a metadata project to identify and catalog hidden sensitive data.

- The *Chief Revenue Officer* may partner with the CDO to improve the quality of customer and prospect data within the CRM application.

- The *Chief Marketing Officer* may co-sponsor a customer master data management project with the CDO for cross-sell and up-sell purposes.

- The *Chief Supply Chain Officer* may co-sponsor an initiative with the CDO to establish a consistent set of product hierarchies.

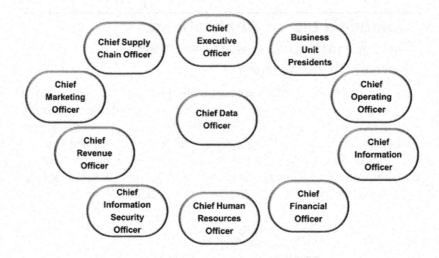

Figure 4.1: CDO stakeholder map

Agree on the Responsibilities of the Data Owner

As part of the chief data office, the data governance team must identify data owners who are accountable for the trustworthiness as well as supporting the security and privacy of data within their purview. For example, the vice president of marketing may be the owner for customer data. The data owner has ultimate accountability for the following tasks relative to the data within his or her purview:

- *Business data stewards*—Appoint business data stewards who manage activities on a day-to-day basis.

- *Data trustworthiness*—Identify critical data elements, agree on business terms, establish business rules, resolve data issues, and improve the quality of data.

- *Security and privacy*—Agree on what constitutes sensitive data, approve access to data, and manage re-validations of data access on a periodic basis.

- *Data monitoring and enforcement*—Monitor the ongoing performance of the data governance program, attend meetings, and answer to internal audit for any lapses in the abovementioned activities.

Compile a List of Applications, Data Repositories, and Datasets Across the Enterprise

As a first step, the data governance team must compile a list of applications, data repositories, and datasets across the enterprise. Table 4.1 shows a sample list of applications, data repositories, and datasets at a large multi-line insurer that offered life, homeowners, and auto insurance. The list includes PolicyCenter for policy management, ClaimCenter for claims management, the enterprise data warehouse (EDW), Facebook data, and the general ledger for subsidiary A.

Table 4.1: Sample applications, data repositories, and datasets at a large multi-line insurer
Application, repository, or dataset
PolicyCenter
ClaimCenter
EDW
Facebook
General Ledger in Subsidiary A

Identify Data Owners Who Are Willing and Able to Be Accountable for Data Within Their Purview

The data governance team must then identify data owners. These data owners may be organized across multiple dimensions:

- *By application or data repository*

  This is the most popular way to organize data owners. For example, the Salesforce CRM™ application may be owned by the vice president of sales operations, and the product catalog may be owned by the vice president of merchandising at a retailer. Mega applications such as SAP® software and the enterprise data warehouse may need to have ownership by subject area, such as customer, vendor, and materials.

- *By department*

  Some companies may classify data owners by department, such as risk management and finance in banking.

- *By dataset including master data and reference data*

  This is also a popular way to classify data owners. For example, the vice president of procurement may be the owner of vendor master data. Also, the vice president of risk management in a bank may be the owner for reference data relating to industry classification codes that drive exposure calculations.

- *By big data type*

  Data owners may also be classified by big data type. For example, the vice president of marketing may be the owner of Facebook and Twitter® data at a retailer. The vice president of equipment may be the owner of sensor data at a railroad operator. Finally, the vice president of claims may be the owner of text analytics from claims adjusters' notes in insurance. This approach to data ownership is a subset of the earlier category by dataset. However, we have called it out separately due to the current focus on big data.

- *By business process*

  Data owners may also be identified for critical business processes, such as order-to-cash, procure-to-pay, or customer on-boarding.

- *By geography*

  Data owners may also be identified by geography. For example, a large oil and gas company had data owners for the North Sea, Gulf of Mexico, and Asia Pacific regions.

- *By some combination of the abovementioned approaches*

  Most companies will adopt some combination of the above-mentioned approaches when establishing their approach to data ownership. Following on from the earlier example, Table 4.2 shows a data ownership matrix at the insurer. Jane is the vice president of policy administration and is the data owner for the PolicyCenter application. Other applications also have data owners, with the exception that the data ownership of the EDW is broken out by subject area.

Table 4.2: Data owners at a large multi-line insurer		
Application, repository, or dataset	Data owner	Title
PolicyCenter	Jane	VP, Policy Administration
ClaimCenter	Jack	VP, Claim Operations
EDW – Customer	Susan	Director of Marketing
EDW – Billing	Sally	Director of Billing Operations
Facebook	Paul	Director of Social Marketing
General Ledger in Subsidiary A	Peter	Manager of Accounting (Subsidiary A)

Obtain Buy-In from Data Owners That They Are Accountable for the Trustworthiness of Data Under Their Ownership

As part of the chief data office, the data governance team must hold data owners accountable for the trustworthiness of data under their ownership. The data owner will typically delegate day-to-day responsibilities to one or more business data stewards. Even if the day-to-day tasks are delegated, the data owner will still maintain accountability for the following tasks:

- *Business glossary*—Create a glossary of definitions of key business terms. This glossary will also include a data dictionary with definitions of column names for key data repositories.

- *Critical data elements*—Identify critical data elements that drive operating performance, financial reporting, or regulatory compliance.

- *Business rules*—Maintain business rules for critical data elements.

- *Data quality*—Improve the quality of data, including the creation of scorecards and handling exceptions.

Agree with Data Owners That They Are Accountable for Supporting Security and Privacy Relative to Data Under Their Ownership

The data governance team must also hold data owners accountable to work with information security to support the security and privacy of data under their ownership. This involves identifying sensitive data such as U.S. Social Security numbers, trade secrets, and financial information.

It also involves managing access to data under their ownership. For example, the vice president of marketing may be the owner for customer data. The data owner must appoint a data steward who will work with information security to identify sensitive data. The data steward must approve access requests to customer data within repositories such as the master data management (MDM) hub. The data steward should also revalidate data access by current users on an annual basis. The data steward may use the following criteria when evaluating requests:

- What business needs require users to view customer data?

- Do users need to view only a subset of screens or data fields? For example, customer service representatives need to view the last four digits of the customer's Social Security number. However, marketing analysts do not need access to this information when calculating the next best offer.

- Do users need to view masked or unmasked data? For example, MDM developers need to work with unmasked customer data as they fine-tune the matching algorithms. However, marketing analysts may not need to view unmasked data.

Ensure That Data Owners Appoint Business Data Stewards to Manage Data on a Day-to-Day Basis

Data ownership is a critical discipline that has a number of responsibilities. Because most data owners are senior executives with busy schedules, the data governance team must ensure that data owners appoint business data stewards to govern data on a day-to-day basis. A business data steward ideally reports into the business and, by virtue of his or her deep subject-matter expertise, is responsible for improving the trustworthiness and safeguarding the privacy of data as an enterprise asset.

Business data stewards have the following responsibilities:

- Data quality management
  - o Identify critical data elements.
  - o Define business rules based on critical data elements.
  - o Resolve data issues uncovered by data profiling.

- Metadata management
  - o Add and modify the definitions for business terms.
  - o Associate business rules with business terms.
  - o Associate reference data with business terms.
  - o Associate business terms with table and column names.
- Master data management
  - o Identify matching attributes.
  - o Create match rules.
  - o Resolve duplicate suspects.
  - o Add and modify hierarchies and groupings.
- Reference data management (RDM)
  - o Add, modify, and delete code values and code tables.
  - o Map code values between code tables in different applications.
- Security and privacy
  - o Define sensitive data.
  - o Flag sensitive data in the metadata repository.
  - o Validate access by users to key systems.
  - o Revalidate access by users to key systems.
  - o Provide input into the acceptable use of data based on business needs, regulatory compliance, and brand reputation.

Table 4.3 expands the earlier tables to also map the business data stewards to each application, data repository, and dataset.

Table 4.3: Data owners and business data stewards at a large multi-line insurer			
Application, repository, or dataset	Data owner	Title of data owner	Business data steward
PolicyCenter	Jane	VP, Policy Administration	Lizzie
ClaimCenter	Jack	VP, Claim Operations	Maya
EDW – Customer	Susan	Director of Marketing	Rhea
EDW – Billing	Sally	Director of Billing Operations	Sasha
Facebook	Paul	Director of Social Marketing	Tara
General Ledger in Subsidiary A	Peter	Manager of Accounting (Subsidiary A)	Laila

Work with the CIO So That Technical Data Stewards Are Accountable for the Data Infrastructure

As discussed in Chapter 3, the scope of the chief data office may vary depending on the extent of the EDM technical infrastructure that remains with the CIO. In all situations, it is important for the CDO to forge a tight working relationship with the CIO. However, doing so is even more important when the CIO retains the bulk of the EDM technical infrastructure. In this situation, IT must appoint technical data stewards to support the activities of the business data stewards. Technical data stewards are also known as data custodians or IT data stewards. Technical data stewards have the following responsibilities:

- Data quality management
  - o Create SQL expressions based on business rules that are defined by the business data stewards.
  - o Provide the appropriate connectivity to source systems for data profiling.
  - o Create workflows so that data exceptions are routed to the appropriate business data stewards for resolution.
- Metadata management
  - o Add, modify, and delete categories for business terms, business rules, and other data artifacts in the metadata repository.
  - o Create workflows so that business terms and business rules are routed to the appropriate stakeholders for approval.
  - o Add or delete users from the metadata repository.
  - o Add, modify, or delete permissions for users in the metadata repository.
  - o Bring technical metadata for relational databases, data integration tools, reports, analytics tools, and data models into the metadata hub.
- Master data management
  - o Add or delete users in the MDM hub.
  - o Add, modify, and delete permissions for users in the MDM hub.

  o Add and drop data stewards from the MDM hub.

  o Create workflows to handle exceptions.

  o Implement matching rules based on input from business data stewards.

 • Reference data management

  o Add or delete users in the RDM hub.

  o Add, modify, and delete permissions for users in the RDM hub.

  o Add and drop data stewards from the RDM hub.

  o Create workflows to handle exceptions.

  o Propagate changes in code values in the RDM hub to source systems.

 • Security and privacy

  o Implement data discovery tools to uncover hidden sensitive data.

  o Implement data masking and data encryption tools.

  o Implement database monitoring tools.

Table 4.4 extends the earlier example to also show the technical data steward for each application, data repository, and dataset.

Table 4.4: Data owners, business data stewards, and technical data stewards at a large multi-line insurer				
Application, repository, or dataset	Data owner	Title of data owner	Business data steward	Technical data steward
PolicyCenter	Jane	VP, Policy Administration	Lizzie	Hubert
ClaimCenter	Jack	VP, Claim Operations	Maya	Cecilia
EDW – Customer	Susan	Director of Marketing	Rhea	Helena
EDW – Billing	Sally	Director of Billing Operations	Sasha	Nisha
Facebook	Paul	Director of Social Marketing	Tara	Mike
General Ledger in Subsidiary A	Peter	Manager of Accounting (Subsidiary A)	Laila	Savio

Identify Operational Data Stewards

The data governance team must also identify operational data stewards, as appropriate. Operational data stewards generally produce data on a day-to-day basis as part of their daily operations. Operational data stewards often have different priorities from business data stewards and data owners. For example, marketing needs high-quality data as the owner of customer data. However, customer service representatives may inadvertently create duplicate customer records while on the phone with the customer. Customer service representatives are often measured on metrics such as average handle time for calls. As a result, the data owner and business data steward from marketing need to work with operational data stewards in customer service to implement policies such as "search before create." This data policy requires the customer service representatives to search for a customer record before creating a new one. The CDO has a key role to reconcile the conflicting objectives of the data owner in marketing (pristine customer data) with those of the operational data stewards in customer service (average call-handling time).

Going back to Case Study 2.1, we will identify the key roles for customer data governance at the retailer:

- *Data owner*—The vice president of marketing was the owner of customer data.

- *Business data steward*—The director of marketing provided business rules to reject dummy phone numbers at the point of sale.

- *Technical data steward*—The director of applications fine-tunes and implements the data validation rules in the point-of-sale software.

- *Operational data steward*—The vice president of store operations required store associates to improve the quality of phone number collections at the point of sale.

Summary

In this chapter, we reviewed a CDO stakeholder map. We also reviewed the responsibilities of a data owner, business data steward, technical data steward, and operational data steward. We highlighted the fact that technical data stewards are critical when IT retains control over the bulk of the EDM technical infrastructure. We walked through an example where we mapped these roles to a list of sample applications, data repositories, and datasets.

5

Setting Data Policies, Standards, and Processes

THE CDO NEEDS TO ESTABLISH A FRAMEWORK TO DOCUMENT the decisions from the data governance program. In this chapter, we will discuss how the chief data office can set data policies, standards, and processes.

Prescribe Terminology for Data Policies

A number of terms—such as data policies, standards, processes, guidelines, and principles—are used to describe data decisions. The CDO must prescribe a consistent terminology to describe these data decisions. In this book, we use a standard framework of *data policies*, *standards*, and *processes*. These artifacts may be found in many places, including in people's heads or embedded in broader policy manuals. Some organizations document their data policies in Microsoft® Word® or Microsoft PowerPoint® and load the documents to Microsoft SharePoint® or an intranet portal. We begin this chapter with definitions of key terms:

- *Data policies*—Data policies provide a broad framework for how decisions should be made regarding data. Data policies are high-level statements and need more detail before they can be operationalized. Each data policy may be supported by one or more data standards.

- *Data standards*—Data standards provide detailed rules on how to implement data policies.

- *Data processes*—Data processes provide special instructions on how to implement data standards. Each data standard may be supported by one or more data processes.

Data policies, standards, and processes follow a hierarchy as shown in Figure 5.1.

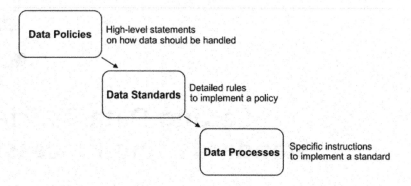

Figure 5.1: Hierarchy of data policies, standards, and processes

Establish a Framework for Data Policies

The CDO must drive a framework for data policies within the following six categories:

1. *By EDM category*—Policies in this category may cover data ownership, data architecture, data modeling, data integration, data security and privacy, master data management, reference data management, metadata management, data quality management, and information lifecycle management.

2. *By data domain*—Policies in this category may cover customer, product, vendor, equipment, and chart of accounts. This category also includes policies to deal with customer duplicates and product hierarchies.

3. *By critical data element*—This data policy includes guidelines to identify critical data elements. Additional policies may cover specific attributes such as U.S. Social Security number, email address, phone number, and product identifier.

4. *By organization*—Policies in this category deal with data issues that are specific to a given function or department, such as risk management or marketing. For example, risk management data policies may deal with the use of data to calculate value at risk. Marketing data policies may address customer segmentation, propensity scores, and contact preferences, such as do not call.

5. *By business process*—Policies in this category may cover customer service and new product introduction. For example, the customer service policy may include a policy that phone representatives need to search for a customer record before creating a new one.

6. *By big data domain*—Policies in this category include the use of big data such as Facebook, Twitter, equipment sensor data, facial recognition, chat logs, and web cookies. We have called out this category separately because there are a number of unique challenges in dealing with these emerging data types.

The remainder of this chapter will review some examples of data policies, standards, and processes.

Data Quality Management Policy

Figure 5.2 shows a hierarchy of policy, standards, and processes for data quality management. The overall data policy includes standards for accountability, critical data elements, and the data quality scorecard. The accountability data standard also refers to the data issue resolution process.

Figure 5.2: Data quality management policy, standards, and processes

Policy

A sample policy for data quality management is shown below:

Data quality management is a discipline that includes the methods to measure and improve the quality and integrity of an organization's data. We must adhere to an enterprise-approved process to manage and improve the quality of business-critical data.

Standards

The data quality management standards are as follows:

- *Accountability*—The data governance team must lead the overall data quality program. However, each data owner must assign one or more business data stewards to manage data quality for key systems and data domains. The responsibilities of the data steward include identifying critical data elements, creating business rules for data profiling, and resolving data issues.

- *Critical data elements*—The data steward must identify critical data elements, which will be the focus of the data quality program. Critical data elements must constitute not more than 10 to 15 percent of the total attributes in a data domain or data repository. These critical data elements must be used to create business rules that will drive the data quality scorecard. For example, "email address should not be null" is a business rule that relates to the "email address" critical data element.

- *Data quality scorecard*—The data governance team must manage a data quality scorecard to track key metrics by system and data domain. This scorecard must be updated on a monthly basis and will be circulated to key stakeholders.

Process

Finally, the accountability data standard links to the data issue resolution process. This process states that the lead data steward must track data issues in a log that will be circulated to stakeholders on a periodic basis. This log must track the list of data issues, severity, assignee, date assigned, and current status.

Metadata Management Policy

Figure 5.3 shows a hierarchy of metadata management policy and standards. The overall metadata management policy refers to the data standards for business glossary, data stewardship, business rules, and data lineage and impact analysis. No data processes have been developed in this case.

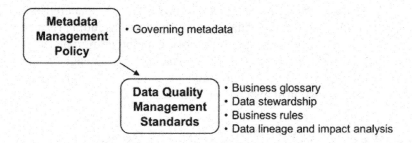

Figure 5.3: Hierarchy of metadata management policy and standards

Policy

The metadata management policy is shown below:

> We must have quality metadata stored within an enterprise metadata repository to manage business terms, technical metadata, business rules, data quality rules, master data rules, reference data, data lineage, and impact analysis.

Standards

The metadata management policy relates to the following metadata management standards:

- *Business glossary*—The data governance team must maintain a business glossary with definitions of key business terms. These business definitions must be created and maintained for critical data elements using organizationally adopted naming and definition standards. The business glossary will also contain a data dictionary with the definitions of column and table names for key data repositories.

- *Data stewardship*—Data owners must assign data stewards to manage business terms and other data artifacts, such as business rules.

- *Business rules*—Business rules for critical data elements must be documented and kept up-to-date for each data repository and must be reflected within the business glossary.

- *Data lineage and impact analysis*—The metadata repository must ingest metadata from key systems, including relational databases, data modeling tools, data integration platforms, reports, analytic models, and Hadoop. The lineage of data elements must be documented and should be up-to-date. Impact analysis must also be performed.

Reference Data Management Policy

Let's review a hierarchy of reference data management policies, standards, and processes. As shown in Figure 5.4, the reference data policy relates to the system of record and stewardship standards. The system of record standard, in turn, relates to the data processes for workflows and propagation.

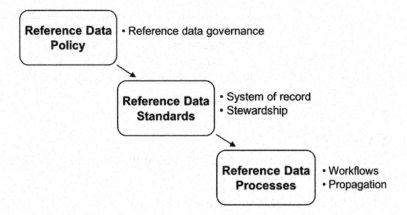

Figure 5.4: Reference data management policy and standards

Policy

The reference data policy is shown below:

> We must identify and manage critical reference data along with the code mappings across critical applications.

Standards

A brief description of the reference data standards is shown below:

- *System of record*—A system of record shall contain an inventory of code tables along with a list of canonical or standard values and a mapping across systems. For example, "AL" is the state code for Alabama. The reference data system of record shall contain this information along with a mapping to state code "1" in another application because Alabama is the first state in an alphabetical list of states.

- *Stewardship*—The EDM team must assign code tables to data owners or data stewards who will be responsible for adding, modifying, and deleting code values.

Processes

The system of record standard relates to the following data processes:

- *Workflows*—Prebuilt workflows must be used to make changes to the code tables. For example, a European country such as "Kosovo" can only be added to the list of country codes based on a recommendation from European finance and approval from global finance.

- *Propagation*—Reference data changes shall be propagated from the reference data hub to target applications across the enterprise. For example, when "Puerto Rico" is added in the state table, the reference data hub will propagate the change as state code "PR" in one application and as state code "51" in another application.

Email Address Policy

Email address may be a critical data element for companies that want to reach a large number of customers electronically. The following topics form part of an overall data policy for email address:

- *Completeness*—The email address field should not be null.

- *Conformity*—Email addresses must be in the format *xxxxx@xxx.xxx*.

- *Uniqueness*—Email addresses must not be duplicated. This business rule addresses situations such as insurance agents entering their own email address in place of a customer's email address. The agents did this to avoid the insurer sending direct emails to the customer; however, the MDM hub inadvertently matched different customers because they shared the same email address.

- *Timeliness*—Customer service representatives should validate email addresses whenever they are on the phone with a customer. An email address is considered stale if it has not been validated in the previous 12 months.

- *Accuracy*—The customer service department should identify any customers with bounced emails. Marketing must validate customer email addresses with external service providers such as Acxiom or Experian® CheetahMail.

Facebook Data Policy

As part of the chief data office, the data governance team must also establish data policies for emerging types of data such as social media. Table 5.1 provides an example of data policies that govern the use of Facebook data within MDM.

Establish Process for Data Policy Changes

As part of the chief data office, the data governance team must establish a process to manage changes to data policies, standards, and processes. The appropriate body, such as the data governance steering committee or data governance council, must approve these changes.

Topic	Relevant Facebook Platform Policies as of March 6, 2012	Implications for MDM
Table 5.1: The implications of Facebook Platform Policies on master data management		
1	A user's friends' data can only be used in the context of the user's experience on your application.	Organizations cannot use data about a person's friends outside the context of the Facebook application (e.g., using Facebook friends to add new relationships within MDM).
2	Subject to certain restrictions, including on transfer, users give you their basic account information when they connect with your application. For all other data obtained through use of the Facebook API, you must obtain explicit consent from the user who provided the data to us before using it for any purpose other than displaying it back to the user on your application.	Organizations need to obtain explicit consent from the user before using any information other than basic account information (name, email, gender, birthday, current city, and the URL of the profile picture).
3	You will not use Facebook user IDs for any purpose outside your application (e.g., your infrastructure, code, or services necessary to build and run your application). Facebook user IDs may be used with external services that you use to build and run your application, such as a web infrastructure service or a distributed computing platform, but only if those services are necessary to running your application and the service has a contractual obligation with you to keep Facebook user IDs confidential.	Organizations need to explore whether they can store Facebook user IDs within MDM.
4	If you stop using Platform or we disable your application, you must delete all data you have received through use of the Facebook API unless: (a) it is basic account information; or (b) you have received explicit consent from the user to retain their data.	Organizations need to be very careful about merging Facebook data with other data within their MDM environment. Consider a situation where an organization merged "married to" information from a user's Facebook profile into their MDM system. If the organization stops using the Facebook Platform, it will need to obtain explicit permission from the user to retain this information. This can be problematic when the organization has merged Facebook data into a golden record that has been propagated across the enterprise.
5	You cannot use a user's friend list outside of your application, even if a user consents to such use, but you can use connections between users who have both connected to your application.	Similar issues to topic 1 above.
6	You will delete all data you receive from us concerning a user if the user asks you to do so, and will provide an easily accessible mechanism for users to make such a request. We may require you to delete data you receive from the Facebook API if you violate our terms.	Similar issues to topic 4 above.

Summary

In this chapter, we reviewed the hierarchy of data policies, standards, and processes. Data policies may be organized by EDM category, data domain, critical data elements, organization, business process, or big data domain. We also walked through sample policies for data quality management, metadata management, reference data management, email address, and Facebook data.

6

Monitoring Data Governance

IN CHAPTER 5, WE DISCUSSED THE FORMULATION OF DATA policies, standards, and processes. However, the CDO needs to add some teeth to the data governance program based on proactive monitoring and enforcement. In this chapter, we will discuss the monitoring of data governance policies, standards, and processes based on dashboards. In Chapter 7, we will review proactive enforcement of data governance policies, standards, and processes.

Data governance monitoring involves regular reporting on the level of compliance to data governance policies, standards, and processes. A data governance dashboard is a useful approach to monitor compliance by relying on peer pressure to improve compliance.

In this chapter, we will review the steps to establish a data governance dashboard. This approach is distinct from a data quality dashboard, which is narrowly focused on the data quality policy.

Select Data Policies, Standards, and Processes to Be Included Within the Dashboard

The first step is to select the data policies, standards, and processes to be included within the dashboard. In Figure 6.1, we have decided to monitor only data governance policies and standards. We have selected three data policies: data security and privacy, metadata, and data quality. Within the data security and privacy policy, we have selected the standards for sensitive data, data discovery, and data masking. Within the metadata policy, we have selected the business glossary and data lineage standards. Finally, within the data quality policy, we have selected the data quality scorecard and data issue resolution standards.

Policy 1 – Data Security & Privacy
1.1 Sensitive data
1.2 Data discovery
1.3 Data masking
Policy 2 – Metadata
2.1 Business glossary
2.2 Data lineage
Policy 3 – Data Quality
3.1 Data quality scorecard
3.2 Data issue resolution

Figure 6.1: Select data governance policies and standards for the dashboard

Pick the Data Repositories to Be Included Within the Dashboard

The dashboard must measure adherence to predefined data policies and standards by data repository. In this case, the dashboard covers Oracle® Financials, Informatica® MDM, Hadoop chat logs, and the Enterprise Data Warehouse as shown in Figure 6.2.

Policy/Standard	Oracle Financials	Informatica MDM	Hadoop Chat Logs	EDW
Policy 1 – Data Security & Privacy				
1.1 Sensitive data				
1.2 Data discovery				
1.3 Data masking				
Policy 2 – Metadata				
2.1 Business glossary				
2.2 Data lineage				
Policy 3 – Data Quality				
3.1 Data quality scorecard				
3.2 Data issue resolution				

Figure 6.2: Select data repositories for the dashboard

Identify Data Owners for Each Policy, Standard, Repository, and Overall

The next step is to identify data owners by data policy, data standard, and data repository and on an overall basis. In Figure 6.3, we have identified business and technology owners at each level. For example, James and Sandra are the overall business and technology owners of the dashboard at the enterprise level.

Policy/ Standard	Business Owner	Technology Owner	Oracle Financials	Informatica MDM	Hadoop Chat Logs	EDW
Business owner	James	Sandra	Sam	Jake	Joan	Bob
Technology owner			Jerry	Peter	Nathan	Weber
Policy 1 – Data Security & Privacy	**Jill**	**John**				
1.1 Sensitive data	Jane	John				
1.2 Data discovery	Sammy	John				
1.3 Data masking	Jill	John				
Policy 2 – Metadata	**John**	**Sally**				
2.1 Business glossary	John	Sally				
2.2 Data lineage	John	Sally				
Policy 3 – Data Quality	**Jack**	**Mary**				
3.1 Data quality scorecard	Jack	Mary				
3.2 Data issue resolution	Jack	Mary				

Figure 6.3: Identify data owners for each policy, standard, repository, and overall

Score Each Data Repository by Data Standard

The data governance team must score each data repository by data standard. As shown in Figure 6.4, the data governance dashboard is based on self-assessment by data owners and uses the following key:

- Limited adherence to data standard = 0 percent

- Partial adherence to data standard = 50 percent

- Broad adherence to data standard = 100 percent

The data governance scores are rolled up on a simple average basis by data policy, by data repository, and for the enterprise. Of course, a more complex scoring is possible on a weighted average basis.

Circulate the Data Governance Dashboard on a Periodic Basis

Finally, the data governance dashboard must be generated on a monthly or quarterly basis. The dashboard must then be circulated to all the business and technology owners. The dashboard must be reviewed with key stakeholders so these executives understand how to interpret the dashboard and appreciate where they could improve from their own business unit perspective.

Summary

In this chapter, we discussed the use of data governance dashboards to monitor data policies, standards, and processes.

Policy/ Standard	Business Owner	Tech- nology Owner	Overall Score	Oracle Financials	Informatica MDM	Hadoop Chat Logs	EDW
Business owner	James	Sandra		Sam	Jake	Joan	Bob
Technology owner				Jerry	Peter	Nathan	Weber
Overall score			**33%**	**53%**	**17%**	**36%**	**28%**
Policy 1 – Data Security & Privacy	**Jill**	**John**	**50%**	**83%**	**50%**	**33%**	**33%**
1.1 Sensitive data	Jane	John	100%	100%	100%	100%	100%
1.2 Data discovery	Sammy	John	13%	50%	0%	0%	0%
1.3 Data masking	Jill	John	38%	100%	50%	0%	0%
Policy 2 – Metadata	**John**	**Sally**	**25%**	**25%**	**0%**	**50%**	**25%**
2.1 Business glossary	John	Sally	50%	50%	0%	100%	50%
2.2 Data lineage	John	Sally	0%	0%	0%	0%	0%
Policy 3 – Data Quality	**Jack**	**Mary**	**25%**	**50%**	**0%**	**25%**	**25%**
3.1 Data quality scorecard	Jack	Mary	50%	100%	0%	50%	50%
3.2 Data issue resolution	Jack	Mary	0%	0%	0%	0%	0%

Figure 6.4: Data governance scorecard shows scores by data standard, data policy, and data repository and on an overall basis

7

Enforcing Data Governance

DATA GOVERNANCE MONITORING IS A SOFTER APPROACH
to ensure compliance with data policies, standards, and processes. On the
other hand, data governance enforcement requires tangible consequences
to non-compliance with data policies, standards, and processes. The CDO
needs to focus on the following topics to enforce data governance policies, standards, and processes.

Determine the Overall Approach to Enforce Data Policies, Standards, and Processes

There are a number of mechanisms to enforce data policies, standards,
and processes:

1. *Business-as-usual escalations to data governance council and
   senior management*

   The data governance department must escalate any instances
   of non-compliance to the data governance council and to senior
   management. This is the most lightweight approach to data governance and reflects business-as-usual.

2. *Regular audits by the data governance team*

   The data governance department may establish a dedicated team
   to audit individual data domains, data repositories, and data owners on a periodic basis. For example, a large bank established a
   dedicated team of 25 individuals who focused on data governance
   audits on an ongoing basis. This approach is less threatening but
   does require a dedicated team. However, it would introduce bias
   because the data governance team would also be required to audit
   itself.

3. *Enforcement by the internal audit department*

The data governance department may also turn over data policies, standards, and processes to the internal audit department. Internal audit can then audit the data governance program as well as individual data owners, data domains, and data repositories. This approach works well in highly regulated industries such as financial services. Such organizations are able to use this approach to demonstrate to regulators that they have the appropriate controls over their data.

Validate Auditability of Data Policies, Standards, and Processes with Internal Audit

Data governance enforcement is workable only if the policies, standards, and processes are auditable. Said differently, an independent party should be able to independently verify adherence to the policies, standards, and processes.

The following is an example of a data standard that is not auditable:

> The company should maintain definitions of key business terms.

On the other hand, the following is an example of a data standard that is auditable:

> The data owner for each data repository is accountable to maintain a data dictionary for key business terms, column names, and table names that should be stored in the metadata repository.

Support Efforts to Audit the Compliance with Data Policies, Standards, and Processes

As discussed earlier, either internal audit or the data governance team must conduct periodic audits to verify compliance with data policies, standards, and processes. The scope of the audit depends on the size and mission of the team that will be doing the audit. For example, the data governance team at a large bank audited 25 percent of the repositories on a quarterly basis with the objective of covering 100 percent of the repositories every year. The nature of the audit depends on the data policies, standards, and processes. However, some of the audit criteria include the following:

- Data ownership

  o Does every data repository have a data owner?

  o Is the data owner listed in the metadata repository?

  o How often does the data owner participate in the meetings of the data governance council?

  o Has the data owner appointed business data stewards to manage activities on a day-to-day basis?

  o How often do the business data stewards participate in the meetings of the data stewardship community?

- Metadata

  o Are critical data elements identified for each data repository? Are they flagged in the metadata repository?

  o Does each data repository have a data dictionary with definitions for critical data elements? Are these definitions included in the metadata repository?

  o Does each data repository have a set of business rules for critical data elements? Are these business rules cataloged in the metadata hub?

  o Is end-to-end data lineage available for critical data elements?

  o How often are the artifacts kept up-to-date by the data stewards?

- Data quality

  o Is data profiling conducted on a periodic basis for each data repository?

  o Is a data quality scorecard produced on a monthly basis for each data repository?

  o Is a data issue resolution process in place for each data repository?

- Security and privacy

  o Does the metadata repository clearly flag sensitive data for each data repository?

  o Do business data stewards validate access for new users to each data repository? If so, are they using preapproved criteria?

  o Do business data stewards revalidate access for existing users to each data repository on an annual basis? If so, are they using preapproved criteria?

Review Deviations from Data Policies, Standards, and Processes

As part of the chief data office, the data governance team must review deviations from data policies, standards, and processes on an ongoing basis. These deviations may be uncovered as part of regular data audits or in the ordinary course of business. The deviations should be reviewed by the data governance steering committee or the data governance council.

Summary

In this chapter, we reviewed how the CDO can add teeth to the data governance program by adding enforcement capabilities. Data governance enforcement includes business-as-usual escalations to the data governance council and senior management, periodic audits by the data governance team, and involvement by internal audit. Data governance policies, standards, and processes must be auditable before they can be enforced. We also reviewed a list of sample criteria that can support a data governance audit.

8

Building a Successful Technology Foundation for Data Governance

A SUCCESSFUL DATA GOVERNANCE PROGRAM REQUIRES strategy, people, process, and technology. It is important for companies to think about these components in that specific order. Many organizations make the mistake of purchasing technology before they have fully defined the strategy, people, and process components of their data governance program. This usually results in problems because the requirements for the technology cannot be clear without first defining the direction of the data governance program.

Once an organization has its strategy, people, and process in place, Informatica provides a robust platform for the technology implementation of data governance. A strong technology platform is critical to successful data governance programs because it can promote collaboration, boost productivity, and enable the repeatable processes that make up data governance. Four of the essential technology pillars of data governance include:

- *Data quality management*

    This capability provides fit-for-purpose tools for IT and business (non-technical) users to discover, understand, and manage the quality of data. It also includes the ability to create scorecards to manage data quality on an ongoing basis, based on metrics defined by the business.

- *Business definitions*

  A business glossary provides the ability for business users to provide business context to the data in terms of term names, definitions, owners, links to relevant documentation and policies, and relationships to other terms.

- *Master data and reference data management*

  A good master data management system helps to discover, manage, and share core data about entities such as customers, part numbers, and partners that is common across applications. Central management of this essential data ensures that it is timely, up-to-date, and consistent across all the systems that use this data.

- *Data flow visibility and change management*

  It is also essential for the organization to have easy visibility into the flow of data across systems. Users should be able to visualize where data comes from, how it is moved, how it is transformed, and where it is ultimately consumed. From an IT perspective, these data flows make it easy to understand and learn the environment and to avoid errors when making changes. From a business perspective, data flows can support regulatory compliance by showing, for example, where the data for a risk calculation came from and how the final risk numbers were produced.

Once data governance requirements have been defined, Informatica should be given strong consideration as the technology platform for several key reasons:

- *Tools for both IT and business users*

  Informatica provides tools with user interfaces that are designed for two classes of users: technical users and non-technical business users. Informatica provides the appropriate interfaces so that users can do their jobs efficiently.

- *Built-in collaboration between business and IT*

  Data governance is by its nature a collaboration between business and IT. Neither group can do the full job without the other, and any attempt by one group to drive a data governance initiative alone will likely fail. Informatica tools incorporate collaboration mechanisms such as task management and messaging to enable collaboration without requiring users to leave the tools they are using.

- *Industry-leading tools in all categories*

  As we discussed earlier, data governance requires multiple tools and user interfaces. Informatica provides tools that are leaders in their respective Gartner® Magic Quadrants.

- *Protection from changes in underlying data technology*

  Informatica is unique with tools that share a common runtime environment. As a result, users who create logic and rules are insulated from changes in the underlying data-persistence technology. In layman's terms, this means that a data transformation created to run on a local SQL database can also be run in the cloud, on a data warehouse appliance, or on a Hadoop cluster without modification. This means people and logic apply consistently across many technologies, boosting productivity and cutting costs.

- *Connectivity to virtually any data source*

  Because Informatica is totally focused on the business of enterprise data management, it has the ability to connect to and access data from virtually any source. As a company business seeks to incorporate partner data, cloud data, social data, mobile data, big data, and data from the Internet of Things, this capability becomes increasingly important.

Summary

Looking forward, the ultimate goal of data governance is to help the organization deliver business value faster and with greater accuracy. A strong technology platform that is adaptable to changes in the technology environment is essential to provide the agility required to meet the needs of the business.

Acronyms

API	Application Programming Interface
BCBS	Basel Committee on Banking Supervision
CDE	Critical Data Element
CDO	Chief Data Officer
CEO	Chief Executive Officer
CIO	Chief Information Officer
CMO	Chief Marketing Officer
COO	Chief Operating Officer
CRO	Chief Risk Officer
EDM	Enterprise Data Management
EDW	Enterprise Data Warehouse
EIM	Enterprise Information Management
FINRA	Financial Industry Regulatory Authority
ILM	Information Lifecycle Management
MDM	Master Data Management
NoSQL	Not Only SQL
SDLC	Systems Development Lifecycle
SQL	Structured Query Language

B

Glossary

Business data steward

A person who ideally reports into the business and, by virtue of his or her deep subject-matter expertise, is responsible for improving the trustworthiness and safeguarding the privacy of data as an enterprise asset.

Business glossary

A repository with definitions of key terms that brings together common definitions across business and IT. A business glossary is often distinguished from a data dictionary, which contains the descriptions of key columns and tables.

Chief Data Office

An EDM department or organization, which reports to the CDO.

Chief Data Officer (CDO)

A C-level executive with overall accountability for enterprise data management.

Content management

The process of digitizing, collecting, and classifying paper and electronic documents.

Critical data element (CDE)

An attribute that has a significant impact on regulatory reporting, operational performance, and business intelligence.

Data architecture

A discipline that sets data standards for data systems as a vision or a model of the eventual interactions between those data systems.[1]

Data dictionary

See business glossary.

Data discovery

The process of discovering data in a system including hidden relationships with other data and hidden values such as U.S. Social Security Numbers in text fields.

Data governance

The formulation of policy to optimize, secure, and leverage information as an enterprise asset by aligning the objectives of multiple functions.

Data governance council

A body consisting of senior business and IT representatives that sets policy regarding information and acts as the ultimate tiebreaker if lower-level bodies cannot make decisions.

Data governance dashboard

A scorecard that displays the degree of compliance with data policies and standards at a point in time and over time.

Data governance enforcement

A process that requires tangible consequences to non-compliance with data policies, standards, and processes.

Data governance lead

The operational leader who leads the data governance program on a day-to-day basis.

Data governance monitoring

A process that involves regular reporting on the level of compliance to data governance policies, standards, and processes.

Data integration

A process that involves combining data from multiple sources to provide new insights to business users.

---

[1] http://en.wikipedia.org/wiki/Data_architecture

Data lineage

The audit trail for data movement through integration processes. The result of a data lineage process is the answer to basic questions such as "Where did this data come from?" and "Where does this data go?" and "What happened to it along the way?"

Data masking

The process of systematically transforming confidential data elements, such as trade secrets and personally identifiable information, into realistic, but fictionalized, values.

Data model

A wayfinding tool for both business and IT professionals, which uses a set of symbols and text to precisely explain a subset of real information to improve communication within the organization and thereby lead to a more flexible and stable application environment.[2]

Data modeling

The process of creating a data model.

Data owner

The individual who is accountable for the trustworthiness as well as supporting security and privacy of data within his or her purview.

Data policy

An artifact that provides a broad framework for how decisions should be made regarding data. A data policy is a high-level statement and needs more detail before it can be operationalized. Each data policy may be supported by one or more data standards.

Data process

An artifact that provides special instructions on how to implement data standards. Each data standard may be supported by one or more data processes.

Data profiling

The process of understanding the data in a system, where it is located, and how it relates to other systems. This process includes developing a statistical analysis of the data, such as data type, null percentages, and uniqueness.

---

[2] *Data Modeling Made Simple 2nd Edition* (Steve Hoberman, Technics Publications, LLC, 2009).

Data quality management

A discipline that includes methods to measure and improve the quality and integrity of an organization's data. While data profiling uncovers issues with the data, data quality actually remediates those issues.

Data quality scorecard

A report that displays the quality of data at a point in time or over time.

Data repository

A database, application, or other location where data is stored electronically.

Data standard

An artifact that provides detailed information on how to implement a data policy. Each data policy may be supported by one or more data standards. Each data standard may be supported by one or more data processes.

Data steward

See business data steward.

Dataset

A collection of data, such as customer contacts, orders, billings, Facebook likes, and Tweets.

Enterprise Data Management (EDM)

The ability of an organization to precisely define, easily integrate, and effectively retrieve data for both internal applications and external communication. It includes a number of disciplines, including data governance, data ownership, data architecture, data modeling, data integration, database management and operations, data security and privacy, master data management, reference data management, data warehousing, critical data elements, metadata management, data quality management, information lifecycle management, and content management.[3]

Enterprise Information Management (EIM)

See Enterprise Data Management.

---

[3] http://en.wikipedia.org/wiki/Enterprise_data_management

Hadoop

Open source software to enable the distributed processing of large data sets across clusters of computers using a simple programming model.

Information Lifecycle Management (ILM)

The process and methodology of managing information through its lifecycle, from creation through disposal, including compliance with legal, regulatory, and privacy requirements.

MapReduce

A computational paradigm in which an application is divided into self-contained units of work. MapReduce applications can process vast amounts (multiple terabytes) of data in parallel on large clusters in a reliable, fault-tolerant manner.

Master Data Management (MDM)

The process of establishing a single version of the truth for an organization's critical data entities, such as customers, products, materials, vendors, and chart of accounts.

Metadata

Information that describes the characteristics of any data artifact, such as its name, location, criticality, quality, business rules, and relationships to other data artifacts.

NoSQL database

A database management system that does not use SQL as its primary query language. The database might not require fixed table schemas and does not support JOIN operations. NoSQL ("not only SQL") databases include categories such as key-value stores. These databases are optimized for highly scalable read-write operations rather than for consistency.

Operational data steward

A person who reports into an operational area, such as customer service or sales operations, and is involved in the creation of data within source systems.

Pig

A platform for analyzing large, semi-structured datasets in Hadoop. Apache Pig uses a procedural language called Pig Latin that insulates users from learning the intricacies of MapReduce programming in Java®.

Propagation

The process of reflecting any changes to data back to the source systems.

Reference data management

The process of managing static data such as country codes, state or province codes, and industry classification codes, which may be placed in lookup tables for reference by other applications across the enterprise.

Systems development lifecycle (SDLC)

The end-to-end lifecycle that involves planning, designing, testing, and deploying information systems.

System of record

A data repository with a single version of the truth for a data entity such as customer, vendor, product, or chart of accounts.

Technical data steward

A technical role that supports the business data steward with tasks such as data profiling, administering the business glossary, adding/modifying/deleting code values, and modifying master data hierarchies.

Tollgate

A project checkpoint where stakeholders determine whether the milestones of the current phase have been achieved and whether it is appropriate to move to the next phase.

Workflow

A chained series of people and system tasks to accomplish a goal. For example, workflows might exist for data issue management, adding a business term, or simple approval.

Key Data Governance Activities on the Agenda of the Chief Data Officer

1. Agree on the reporting relationship for the CDO

2. Determine the level of centralization of the chief data office

3. Define the overall scope of the chief data office

4. Establish overall funding and decision-making authority

5. Enlist the Chief Information Officer as a strong partner

6. Appoint a data governance lead

7. Establish a data governance program office

8. Build a stakeholder map

9. Agree on the responsibilities of the data owner

10. Compile a list of applications, data repositories, and datasets across the enterprise

11. Identify data owners who are willing and able to be accountable for data within their purview

12. Obtain buy-in from data owners that they are accountable for the trustworthiness of data under their ownership

13. Agree with data owners that they are accountable for supporting security and privacy relative to data under their ownership

14. Ensure that data owners appoint business data stewards to manage data on a day-to-day basis

15. Work with the CIO so that technical data stewards are accountable for the data infrastructure

16. Identify operational data stewards

17. Prescribe terminology for data policies

18. Establish a framework for data policies

19. Sample data quality management policy

20. Sample metadata management policy

21. Sample reference data management policy

22. Sample email address policy

23. Sample Facebook data policy

24. Establish process for data policy changes

25. Select data policies, standards, and processes to be included within the data governance dashboard

26. Pick the data repositories to be included within the data governance dashboard

27. Identify data owners for each policy, standard, repository, and overall within the data governance dashboard

28. Score each data repository by data standard within the data governance dashboard

29. Circulate the data governance dashboard on a periodic basis

30. Determine the overall approach to enforce data policies, standards, and processes

31. Validate auditability of data policies, standards, and processes with internal audit

32. Support efforts to audit the compliance with data policies, standards, and processes

33. Review deviations from data policies, standards, and processes